ANIMALS AT WORK

Animals Communicating

WORLD BOOK

World Book, Inc.
180 North LaSalle Street
Suite 900
Chicago, Illinois 60601
USA

Produced for World Book, Inc. by Bailey Publishing Associates Ltd.

For information about other World Book publications, visit our website at **www.worldbook.com** or call **1-800-WORLDBK (967-5325)**.

Library of Congress Cataloging-in-Publication data has been applied for.

Title: Animals Communicating
ISBN: 978-0-7166-2727-2

Animals at Work
ISBN: 978-0-7166-2724-1 (set, hc)

Also available as:
ISBN: 978-0-7166-2740-1 (e-book)

1st printing August 2018

Staff

Writer: Mary Auld

Executive Committee

President
Jim O'Rourke

Vice President and Editor in Chief
Paul A. Kobasa

Vice President, Finance
Donald D. Keller

Vice President, Marketing
Jean Lin

Vice President, International
Maksim Rutenberg

Vice President, Technology
Jason Dole

Director, Human Resources
Bev Ecker

Editorial

Director, Print Publishing
Tom Evans

Managing Editor
Jeff De La Rosa

Editor
William D. Adams

Manager, Contracts & Compliance
(Rights & Permissions)
Loranne K. Shields

Manager, Indexing Services
David Pofelski

Librarian
S. Thomas Richardson

Digital

Director, Digital Product
Development
Erika Meller

Digital Product Manager
Jonathan Wills

Manufacturing/Production

Manufacturing Manager
Anne Fritzinger

Proofreader
Nathalie Strassheim

Graphics and Design

Senior Art Director
Tom Evans

Senior Designer
Don Di Sante

Media Editor
Rosalia Bledsoe

Special thanks to:

Roberta Bailey
Nicola Barber
Francis Paola Lea
Claire Munday
Alex Woolf

Two red wood ants communicating in eastern Russia. Ants share information through touch and chemicals called pheromones.

Acknowledgments

Cover photo: © Andrey Pavlov, Shutterstock

Alamy: title page & 41 (indiaforte), 8-9 (Thorsten Negro/imageBROKER), 9 (Paulo Oliveira), 10-11 (WildPictures), 12-13 (Avalon/Photoshot License), 14-15 (Gilles Barbier/imageBROKER), 15 (David Keith Jones/Images of Africa Photobank), 18-19 (Evgeni Ivanov), 19 (Sabena Jane Blackbird), 22-23 (Joe Quinn), 28-29 (Ann and Steve Toon), 29 (Aleksey Suvorov), 31 (Ryan McGinnis), 32-33 (Kelvin Aitken/VWPics), 36 (Ernie Janes), 39 (Vivek Gour-Broome/ephotocorp), 42-43 (Scott Camazine). **Shutterstock**: 5 (Thomas Barrat), 6-7 (dimakig), 7 (Kseniya Lanzarote), 8 (SeraphP), 10 (Michal Pesata), 11 (duangnapa_b), 13 (MediaFuzeBox), 16-17 (Brian Lasenby), 17 (Victor Tyakht), 20 (Victor Tyakht), 20-21 (Louis Freeman), 21 (Oleg Znamenskiy), 22 (Aria_RJWarren), 23 (Ryan M. Bolton), 24-25 (Rudmer Zwerver), 25 (Tatiana Grozetskaya), 27 (Martin Prochazkacz), 32 (Matt Jeppson), 33 (reptiles4all), 34-35 (Anastasija Popova), 35 (Anteromite), 36-37 (Neil Bradfield), 37 (Kuttelvaserova Stuchelova), 38-39 (Leonardo Gonzalez), 43 (timsimages), 45 (Soloviova Liudmyla).

Contents

4   Introduction

6   Visual Communication

16   Using Sound

28   Scents and Smells

34   Touch and Feel

42   Studying Animal Communication

46   Glossary

47   Find Out More

48   Index

Introduction

Communication is the giving and getting—exchanging—of information. In communication, someone or something sends out a message, and another receives it. Humans communicate with each other all the time. Sometimes we communicate face to face. Other times, we communicate at a distance by telephone or computer network. Communication can be as simple as a facial expression or as complex as the combination of sounds or signs we call **language.**

Animals communicate all the time, too. Sometimes they communicate to members of their own **species,** and at other times they communicate with other kinds of animals. Animals exchange information using their senses of sight, hearing, smell, taste, and touch. Some animals use one sense more than another to communicate, and many use their senses in combination.

For animals, communication is all about survival. Animals exchange messages to warn each other of danger, to tell each other where to find food, to protect their **territory** or their young, and also to find a **mate.** Mating is an important part of survival. It makes the next generation so that the species can continue.

Humans have developed some amazing ways of communicating—not just through spoken language, but also through writing words and numbers. No other animal uses these methods. But many animals have developed some amazing ways of communicating, sometimes using senses far more developed than those of humans and sometimes exchanging far more complex information than we might imagine. Indeed, some scientists think that some animals have developed ways of communicating that are in some ways like human language.

In this book, you will learn some of the ways and reasons animals communicate, from the simple exchange of warning signals to complex, language-like calls.

Wolves are famous for their howls. The howl of a wolf tells other wolves where it is. A pack of wolves howls together to keep other wolves off its territory.

Visual Communication

Few animals are completely blind, so vision—seeing—is an important part of how many animals gather information about the world. Many **species** communicate using visual signals. Some animals have better eyesight than others, allowing for complex visual communication. Birds, for example, see in color. Showing and recognizing bright colors is part of their way of exchanging information.

ATTRACTIVE COLORS

A female bird often chooses her **mate** based on the color and condition of the male's **plumage** (*PLOO mihg;* feathers). This shows her that the male is healthy and has a good diet. To attract the female's attention, the plumage of the males is more brightly colored than that of females in many species. When it is time to mate, males often display—show off—their feathers. The male who best communicates his fitness through the display of his plumage is more likely to win a mate.

LOOK OUT—DANGER

Colors can also give out another message: back off. The bright red of a ladybug's wings sends a warning to would-be **predators** that the **insect** contains a foul-tasting chemical. The more brightly colored the species of ladybug, the more poison its body contains. The brilliant colors of poison dart frogs, which live in the Amazon rain forest, warn predators that eating them is dangerous. The frogs' name comes from a poison found in their skin, which local people traditionally use to add poison to their weapons to make them more deadly.

A colorful male pheasant shows off his feathers to attract a mate.

Protective stripes

Wasps and bees are known for their black and yellow stripes, which warn other animals of their sting. Hoverflies have stripes like bees and wasps, but have no sting. But because they **mimic** stinging insects, **predators** avoid them, too.

A hoverfly's coloring mimics that of wasps and bees.

CHANGING COLORS

A male bird's **plumage** changes with its age, and the colors often get brighter during the **mating** season. Like birds, some fish change color when they are ready to mate. The male stickleback's color change is among the most dramatic. Each spring, when the fish are preparing to **spawn,** the male's silvery body becomes increasingly red or orange. This color change tells the females that the male is ready to mate.

Color changes slowly in most animals, but other animals communicate through quick color changes. For many years, for example, people thought chameleons changed color to blend in with their surroundings. But research has shown that their color changes are more a reflection of mood—how they are feeling. Bright reds and yellows show other chameleons that they are angry or looking to mate. Darker colors communicate that a chameleon is not a threat and will not fight.

Some **invertebrate** sea creatures, such as octopuses, squid, and cuttlefish, have skin that can change color instantly to match their surroundings. This ability keeps them safe and gives them an edge when hunting. They also use this ability to communicate with—and even to trick—each other. Giant cuttlefish males, for example, take on blue edge colors when ready to mate. But some smaller males change their color to look like the females. This trick allows them to sneak up on the females without the larger males noticing!

This male giant cuttlefish has a blue edge, showing that it is ready to mate.

Chameleons turn bright
colors when they are
ready to mate or fight.

Bioluminescence

Some animals are **bioluminescent,**
meaning they make their own light. The
firefly lights up using a chemical reaction
in its body. Its flashes give out different
messages. In the **larvae,** the flashes warn
predators that they taste nasty. In adults,
they help in finding mates—the females
are attracted to particular flash patterns.

A male firefly creates
patterns of flashes
to attract a mate.

MOVEMENTS

Body movements can also be used to communicate visually. Humans often use hand movements, also called gestures, but animals may gesture using other parts of their bodies. A house cat, for example, may twitch its tail when it is unhappy or angry. An elephant may use the position of its trunk to communicate (see page 40).

Some gestures begin in animals from the earliest ages. Most baby birds beg for food from their parents by opening up their beaks wide. The parents know the chick is hungry, and usually the wider a beak is open, the more likely the chick will be fed before its brothers and sisters.

Chimpanzees are closely related to humans, so perhaps it is not surprising that they too use hand gestures to communicate. So when a chimp scratches itself in front of another, it is signaling the other chimp that it wants to be **groomed.** Chimps have more flexible feet than humans and use them to gesture, too—a mother will nudge her baby with her foot to tell it to climb on her back.

Researchers have seen ravens using their beaks to show things, such as moss, stones, and twigs, to other ravens, usually of the opposite sex. The other raven will often look at the object and might pick it up as well. These actions might be a type of bonding display–getting to know each other–before mating.

Shaking a claw

In the male fiddler crab, one claw is much larger than the other. This big claw is useful for waving, drumming against its other claw, and attracting females. Researchers have found females choose the males with the largest claw that drums the loudest, as it shows the male is strong and will make a good father.

MAKING FACES

Humans often pick up signals from each other through our facial expressions—how we make our faces look, by smiling or frowning, for example. Other **mammals** also use this way of communicating. Mammals have more face muscles than other animals because when they are babies, they need them to suck milk from their mother's body. These muscles also allow mammals to use complex facial expressions. One well-known expression is a chimpanzee's "grin," which looks like a human smile. In fact, this look is often linked to being nervous or showing **submission,** though there is evidence that chimps do laugh and smile out of happiness, as well.

Dogs and their wild relatives, wolves, have different facial expressions. People often pick up on such expressions with their own pets. A dog with wide-open eyes and a relaxed face could be gazing lovingly at its owner. A dog with its ears pricked and eyes focused is alert to something. In fact, dogs have more known expressions than wolves, likely because of their long history with humans. But both animals clearly communicate by watching and holding eye contact.

Some expressions are used on purpose to communicate, while others are instinctive reactions or reflexes. An *instinct* is something an animal is born knowing how to do. For example, most birds instinctively know how to build their nests. A *reflex,* such as blinking at a bright light, is another type of behavior that does not have to be learned but is not as complex as an instinct. An example of a reflex that uses a facial expression is people wincing when they feel pain. This kind of facial expression has been seen in many other mammals, including sheep and mice. Scientists think these expressions may show members of a group that one individual needs support. It may also warn the group of potential danger.

Horses have good eyesight and frequently use facial expressions to communicate. **Zoologists** have identified 17 different facial expressions in horses—more than have been identified in dogs. The different expressions convey different emotional states. A raised inner eyebrow can show sadness. A slight pull of the lip of the mouth shows submission to a stronger horse.

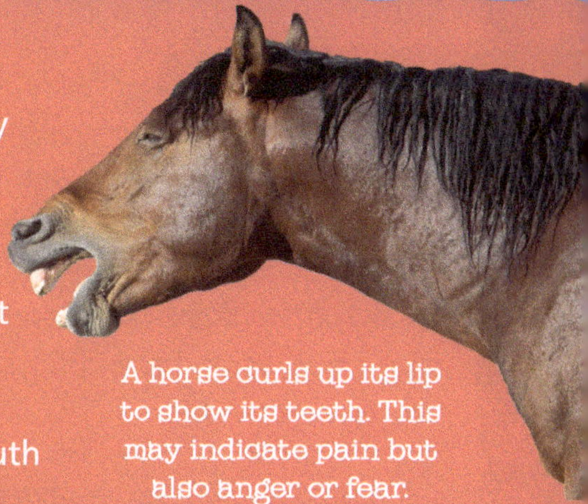

A horse curls up its lip to show its teeth. This may indicate pain but also anger or fear.

A chimpanzee is not necessarily happy when it smiles.

BODY LANGUAGE

Many forms of visual communication involve the whole body. Often, animals make themselves look bigger to intimidate (frighten) other animals. Cats arch their back and their fur stands on end for this reason. Monitor lizards, which often fight over **territory,** food, or **mates,** puff up their bodies and stand up high to make themselves look as large as possible.

DANCING DISPLAYS

A good dancer attracts attention on the dance floor. In the same way, many **species** of bird, such as pheasants, perform elaborate displays to attract a mate, often showing off their colorful **plumage** (see page 6). The males will strut, flap their wings, and leap in the air to encourage a female to choose them. Among bird species that mate for life, such as cranes, a mating couple display together in a ritual that helps build lasting bonds between them. Honey bees live in **colonies** called hives made up of thousands of bees. When a hive becomes overcrowded, some of its bees **swarm** to form a new hive. They begin by sending out scouts to find a suitable place. The returning scouts perform a "dance," waggling their bodies to show the direction of a site they have found. Other scouts investigate, and a site is chosen. Bees also perform similar dances to tell other bees where to find food. When a worker bee finds flowers full of sweet nectar to eat and make honey with, it flies back to the hive and tells other bees where the flowers are.

Stotting gazelle

When lions attack a herd of grazing gazelle, you would expect the first thing the gazelles would do is run away. Instead, some young, fit gazelles pause, springing high in the air with all four feet, before they start to run. This action, called "stotting," shows the lions that the gazelles are healthy. Because the lions are unlikely to catch such fit animals, they may quickly give up the chase, saving both animals energy.

A stotting gazelle shows its fitness to predators.

A monitor lizard rears up on his back legs to make himself look big.

Using Sound

Many animals have a good sense of hearing, so they can use sound to communicate. Some have developed complex sound patterns to exchange messages, such as singing.

FEED ME

Baby animals often call to get the attention of their parents, usually because they are hungry. Among birds, for instance, chicks call constantly for food when a parent is around. Chicks have good reason to call loudly. When food is scarce, a parent might give what little food it can find to the strongest chick, to make sure that at least one of its offspring survives. A chick that is begging loudly for food is likely to be stronger and healthier than one that is calling more softly.

CHECK ME OUT

Animals frequently use calls to attract **mates.** Many male birds call or sing to attract female birds. The call or song is an indicator of the male's quality: a strong voice is a sign of a healthy bird and a good potential father. Many types of male frog also call to draw the attention of females, sometimes gathering in groups near ponds or streams. The males call using their **voice box,** but some **species** also have a vocal sac. The vocal sac is a pouch on the throat that gets bigger when the frog calls, making the noise louder. Female frogs find the males of their species through the call and may make their choice of mate based on voice.

Birdsong

About half of bird species can sing. Most of these are perching birds, a group sometimes simply called **songbirds**. Songbirds have a special **organ** above their lungs called the syrinx. Its sides vibrate to make sound when air passes over them. The syrinx has two parts, so a songbird can sing two notes at once. Birds such as thrushes use this ability to make beautiful music. Usually, only male songbirds sing. Their songs have two main purposes: to mark out their **territory** or to attract a mate. Some birds have different songs for attracting a mate and defining their territory. Others use the same song.

The song of the male thrush nightingale is loud and includes whistles, trills, and clicks.

A male spring peeper frog calling for a mate.

WATCH OUT

Many animals use sound to send an alarm. Alarm calls are often used where threatened animals cannot see each other easily, such as among leafy tree branches. They are also useful when animals are focused on something else, such as eating, rather than watching for danger. Alarm calls have another function—they tell a potential **predator** that the **prey** knows it is there, so it may have better luck looking for food elsewhere.

Vervet monkeys are mainly found in the forests of Southern Africa. They live in close-knit groups that can range from around 10 to 70 animals. **Foraging** groups call to tell each other of danger, and they have different calls for different predators. A short, breathy call indicates a leopard; a low-pitched grunt warns of an eagle; and a high-pitched "chutter" says python. The monkeys react differently according to the call, moving up the trees to avoid a leopard and down to avoid an eagle.

Groups of prairie dogs stand on their hilly burrows to keep an eye out for danger. An alarm call tells other members of the group to return to the safety of the burrow. Mothers usually give these alarm calls to warn their young. The calls seem to get louder later in the summer, perhaps because the young born in spring are now foraging farther from their burrows.

Reptile alert

Alarm calls might be a kind of universal signal among more advanced animals. Scientists think that all land-dwelling **vertebrates** can interpret an excited call made by another type of animal. Such calls often mean that danger is near.

For instance, in Madagascar, an island off Africa, there is a **species** of iguana that is silent but has ears. **Zoologists** think it uses its sense of hearing to pick up on the alarm calls of the Madagascar paradise flycatcher, a bird. Both species are hunted by birds of prey, so the iguana picks up the warnings of the flycatchers and heads for cover.

A spiny-tailed iguana hears a flycatcher's cry of alarm.

Prairie dogs stand on their burrows to watch for danger.

THIS IS MY SPACE

Animals may also call to tell rivals they are around and to warn them to stay away. Male birds often sing in the early morning from tree branches, announcing their claim of the area to other males of the same **species.** Some male frogs also call to tell other male frogs that their particular patch of land is taken, along with the females in it. Other animals, such as lions, also use noise to claim their **territory** by roaring or making some other loud noise. Close up, animals may growl or hiss when a rival, **predator,** or other large animal comes near them. A snake hisses to warn predators or other large animals that it will attack if they come any closer.

Warning calls help animals to avoid fights. An animal will usually only attack a rival or outsider as a last resort. Fights are extremely dangerous: the fighters could get injured or killed. By making territorial or warning calls, animals are giving rivals and outsiders a chance to stay away or retreat before a fight breaks out.

Many kinds of male birds sing partly to mark their territory.

HERE I AM

Animals that live in groups often use sound to tell other animals where they are. A lion's roar can be heard up to 5 miles (8 kilometers) away. While a lion's roar can be a warning, it is also a way of telling other lions in its group, which is called a pride, where it is. Lions often separate from the pride to hunt. Afterwards, they exchange roars so they can find each other again. Calls do not have to be long-distance, though. Geese flying in a close grouping honk to one another to help stay in their places.

Singing families

Gibbons are small **apes** that live in the rain forests of southern Asia. They communicate to their family groups and claim territory through loud calls. The sound echoes well over the rain forest treetops. Gibbons **mate** for life, and couples often sing together, sometimes with their offspring.

BODY NOISES

Animals do not communicate only by using their voices. Just as humans can make a noise by clapping hands, many animals use different parts of their bodies to make sounds. A male gorilla beats its chest as it roars to show it is the **dominant** member of its group. **Insects** have no vocal **organs,** but many rub different parts of their body together to make noise. For example, crickets chirp to attract a **mate** by rubbing their front wings together.

Noise travels well underwater, and many fish communicate with sound. Most bony fish have an organ called a **swim bladder** that helps them control their position in the water. Some fish also use this gas-filled organ to make sounds. Male toadfish vibrate their swim bladders to create dull grunts and hums that attract females. Large groups of toadfish have been known to make so much noise that they disturb people living around the bays in which the fish gather to mate.

PLAYING INSTRUMENTS

A few animals make noises using things other than their bodies. Orangutans are known to shape leaves so that they can be used as a whistle. Woodpeckers drum on trees not to look for food but to mark their **territory.**

A red-bellied woodpecker drums a tree with its beak.

Shaking a tail

A rattlesnake shakes its tail to warn **predators** to keep away, reminding them of its **venomous** bite. The tail is made of scales different from those that cover the snake's body. The scales are hollow and loosely joined, so they rattle against each other when shaken. Some other snakes imitate the rattlesnake, vibrating their tails against grass or leaves. Predators leave these **mimics** alone, too.

A rattlesnake shakes its tail as a warning.

A male oyster toadfish makes a loud sound with its swim bladder to attract females during the mating season.

SUPER SOUND SENSITIVE

Many animals have better hearing than humans and can pick up sounds we miss. A rabbit's long ears, for example, pick up more sounds than ours do. Some animals can hear sounds that people cannot hear at all. There are high-pitched ultrasounds or low-pitched infrasounds that are beyond the range of human hearing.

Some animals use ultrasound to communicate. Male mice attract females with a special ultrasound "song." The longer and more complex the song, the more the females like it. Some moths also communicate to potential **mates** with ultrasonic sounds. But ultrasound does not travel far and can get blocked or changed by objects in between the sound maker and the listener. So, most animals use lower-pitched sounds to communicate.

The lower-pitched a sound is, the farther it can travel. Some animals make use of this fact by communicating through sounds lower than can be heard by the human ear. Elephants use such infrasound to keep track of one another in the huge space of the African **savanna** (see pages 40-41).

Infrasound travels even faster and farther in water. Hippos communicate in the water, even though their mouths and ear flaps are closed (see panel on facing page). Whales can also use infrasounds as part of their calls, which can be heard for many miles or kilometers (see pages 26-27). Other animals, such as snakes and fish, can also sense infrasounds. But only larger animals are capable of making them.

"

Bellows in the water

Male hippos mark their **territory** through bellows (loud, deep noises) heard both out of and in the water. Above, the sound comes out of their nostrils. Below, sound vibrations made in their **voice box** pass out into the water through a layer of fat around their neck. Other hippos in the water pick up these vibrations through their jaws, at a point where they connect to the inner ear.

A hippo's infrasonic calls can be heard both out of and in the water.

Male mice attract mates with ultrasonic calls.

Whale Music

Baleen whales are huge, intelligent **mammals** that live throughout the world's oceans. They eat tiny sea creatures that they strain from the water using plates in their mouth called baleen. The whales generally live alone or in small family groups, but they communictate with each other with deep calls, often including infrasound. These sounds can carry as far as 50 miles (80 kilometers) through the water.

One **species** of baleen (*buh LEEN*) whale, the humpback, uses a complex range of sounds that is often called "whale song." It is the male humpback that sings, with songs lasting up to 20 minutes at a time. The tune is made up of different moans, howls, and cries that vary in pitch and also in volume.

A whale often repeats the same song and hears a very similar one back from other males in the area. Males in a different area sing different tunes. The whales' songs change a little each year. Many **zoologists** think that the whales change their songs on purpose.

So what are the whales communicating with this song? No one knows for sure. The males sing when the humpbacks come together in warmer seas to breed, so it is probably linked to choosing a **mate.** Is a female attracted by the male who sings the best song? Or are the males simply telling other males where they are and to keep their distance? Zoologists continue to research this fascinating subject.

Humpbacks also communicate by breaching. Breaching is when a whale leaps high out of the water, slapping its fins and tail on the surface as it splashes back down, creating a lot of noise. Some scientists now think the whales use breaching to communicate with other humpbacks as they travel to and from their breeding grounds.

Scents and Smells

Many animals have a strong sense of smell and use different scents and smells to communicate. Scents can stay in place for a long time, so animals can use them to claim large areas of **territory,** even if they are not currently nearby.

SOURCES OF SMELL

An animal's urine and feces (*FEE seez;* liquid and solid waste) contain lots of interesting smells, many of which can be decoded by other members of the same **species.** The smells can tell others of the same species where an animal is, whether it is male or female, and whether it is ready to **mate.** For example, when pet dogs urinate (*YUR uh nayt)* on lampposts, they are letting other dogs know that they are around. Groups of rhinoceroses mark their territory with dung middens—huge, communal piles of feces that can be as large as 60 feet (20 meters) across. The middens not only warn away rhinos from other groups, they also serve to pass messages in the rhino group. For example, the **dominant** male may pick up the scent of a female in his group who is ready to mate.

Smells do not only come from urine and feces. Many animals have scent **glands** on their bodies that give out their special identifying smell, sometimes called **musk.** Crocodiles and alligators have four musk glands, two of them beneath their jaws and two lower on the body, near the base of the tail. These **reptiles** use the smells given out by the glands to ward off other rivals and to attract mates. Males often rub the musk glands in their face against the female before mating.

Perfume from animals

Humans have long prized the scent glands of some animals for use in creating their own perfumes. The musk deer of Central Asia was nearly hunted to **extinction** for its prized musk gland. Today, most perfumes make use of artificial musk.

Only male musk deer have musk glands.

Pheromones

Smells are the result of traces of chemical substances in the air. When these chemical substances are given out and sensed by animals as a way to communicate, they are called **pheromones** (*FEHR uh mohnz*). A great many animals—from the tiniest creatures to humans—use pheromones. But most scientists think that humans, with so many other senses in use, pick up on these smell signals without knowing it.

Animals give out different pheromones to communicate different messages. There are alarm pheromones, which signal distress. For example, fish called carp give out these signals when they are injured, warning other fish to keep away. Ants also use pheromones to warn other members of their **colony** about potential danger, signaling them to return to the safety of the nest.

Another set of pheromones is used to help find a source of food. An ant that finds the food returns to the colony, marking its way with trail pheromones that other ants can follow. Flying bees and wasps also use a trail of pheromones to mark the opening of a new nest, helping the worker **insects** to enter.

Animals also use pheromones to send signals involved in **mating.** Male wild boars on the hunt for a mate give out a pheromone from their saliva that female boars find very attractive. Many **species** of male butterfly give off pheromones to attract females to mate. At first, the pheromones may simply tell the female that

the male is from the same species. But they also help the male to approach and mate with the female. Some males perform a **courtship** flight above the female to spread these pheromones.

Humans have used artificial pheromones to control insect pests, such as weevils and gypsy moths, by changing their natural behavior. Farmers spread their crops with these chemicals, and the smells they give out prevent the males from finding mates, stopping the insects from breeding.

SCENT DETECTORS

Many animals have a far better sense of smell than that of humans. **Vertebrates** such as wolves, which need and use smell to communicate or find food, have a larger part of their brain devoted to processing smells.

Most vertebrates have a nose or similar **organ** to pick up smells. For example, the chamois (*SHAM ee),* a mountain goat, senses a **predator** in the area by sniffing the air with its nose. An elephant's trunk is an adapted nose and upper lip, which it uses to smell other elephants and animals around it (see page 40). **Insects** and other **invertebrates** pick up smells with their **antennae** on either side of the head.

Pheromones and other scents spread through water as well as air. Sharks can sniff out their **prey,** such as tuna, at distances of several hundred feet or meters, depending on the direction of the sea current. Sex pheromones are important for sharks and other fish, too. The females give them out, allowing males to find potential **mates** across the ocean depths.

Male giant silkworm moths have antennae with extremely sensitive scent receivers. Some species can smell a female moth's sex pheromone from miles or kilometers away.

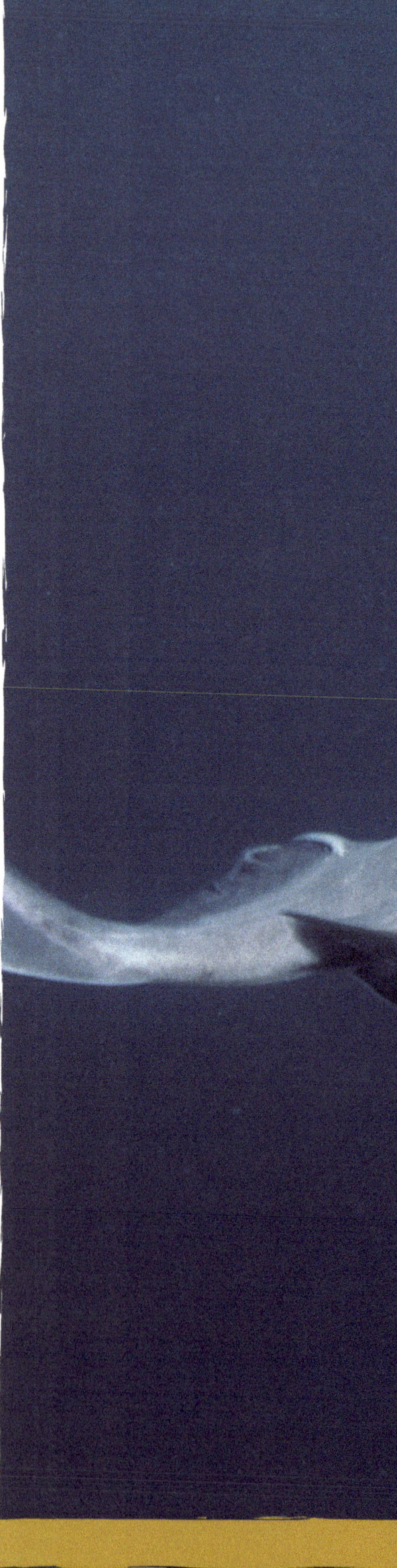

Snakes' smell sensor

Snakes do not smell through their nose. They smell odors with two sacs in their mouth called a Jacobson's organ. They pick up pheromones with their tongue, transferring the tiny bits to the Jacobson's organ as the tongue flicks in and out of their mouth. They find prey and other snakes, including potential mates, in this way.

Touch and Feel

The sense of touch and ability to feel movement are important in animal communication. Like humans, many animals sense touch through their skin or hairs on their bodies. Nerve endings pick up these signals and send them to the brain.

GREETING

Like humans, animals may touch each other in greeting. Greetings may help animals collect information about each other and show that they are not dangerous. Elephants greet one another by intertwining their trunks (see pages 40-41). Cats, pigs, horses, and other animals may touch noses when they meet. Such nose-oriented greetings also allow for sharing of scent information.

COMBAT

Among many **species,** males touch as they fight with rivals to win **mates.** Although these contests can get rough, touching and posturing—bending and turning the body—can often help them to avoid a bad fight. Rivals can gather information about each other's size and strength through touch. If the two differ greatly, the smaller or weaker rival can give up instead of risking injury or death. Male giraffes compete for females by "necking"—standing in front of each other and wrapping their necks together to decide which is **dominant.**

BEFORE MATING

To mate, most animals have to touch, and touch communication may also form part of the activities leading to mating. Seahorses wrap their tails around each other before mating. Alligators and crocodiles rub their sensitive snouts together.

PARENTAL CARE

Animals and their young often communicate through touch. **Mammals** may caress and cuddle their young, sometimes to encourage them to **suckle.** In turn, a baby mammal may press on its mother's mammary **gland** with its forelimbs, causing milk to be made. A gentle nudge from an adult may guide young animals to safety or toward food.

SOCIAL GROOMING

Many animals clean each other in a process called **grooming.**
Grooming may be necessary to keep others clean, such as
when a mother cat cleans her kittens with her tongue. But for
some animals, it has become a social habit and one of the
ways in which they communicate.

Monkeys and **apes** that live in groups often use grooming
as a way of strengthening their **social structure,** such as by
showing that a particular individual is **dominant** over another.
They may also use grooming to make relationships stronger,
such as that between parent and child. Baboons spend over
two hours a day cleaning each other's fur. A study of two
groups of gibbons observed that the group that groomed one
another more often was the more stable of the two.

Birds **preen** their feathers with their beaks to clean them.
Many perform this task for themselves, but some birds preen
each other, often focusing on the head and neck. Some of
this may simply be for the sake of good hygiene—a bird can
not reach that part of its body with its own beak. But there
are other reasons for this behavior, too. Pairs of birds forming
bonds often preen each other. Social preening is also common
between pairs of birds that **mate** and then go on to share
responsibility for raising chicks.

Zoologists have observed that
preening and grooming can also
be used to calm anger. An animal
that wants to avoid a fight will offer
itself for grooming.

Lovebirds preen each
other. They mate for life.

Honey bee cleaners

Honey bees get covered by dust and pollen as they gather food. Some of this gets onto parts of their body they cannot reach, so they use body **language** to ask other bees in the hive to clean it off. This cleaning helps the hive run smoothly.

Honey bees help each other with grooming.

Baboons grooming each other.

VIBRATIONS

Most animals can feel vibrations—in fact, sounds are vibrations in the air or water interpreted through the sense of hearing. But some animals feel vibrations through other parts of their body, and this too can be used as a way of communicating. Several animals pick up vibrations in the ground. When calling for a **mate,** for example, Caribbean white-lipped frogs gather near water and partially bury themselves in the mud. When their vocal sacs get bigger, the sacs hit the ground around them, making it shake. Other males nearby feel the vibrations and know to keep their distance.

WATER MOVEMENTS

Fish feel movements in the water through their **lateral lines,** a row of touch-sensitive grooves that run in a line along either side of their bodies. They help the fish feel the flow of water around them, as well as other objects moving in it. This is one of the reasons they are able to **school.** The lateral lines also warn fish of potential danger outside of their range of vision.

SPIDER WEBS

Spiders that spin webs pick up vibrations in the web through their legs. This lets them know when their **prey** gets caught in their sticky trap, but spiders also use vibration for communication. For example, the male may pluck the female's web as it approaches to mate, letting her know that he is not a tasty meal.

Head-bangers

African termites build huge mounds as homes for their large **colonies.** If a termite senses the approach of a **predator,** it bangs its head on the ground 11 times per second. This banging alerts its nearest neighbors, which begin to bang their heads, too, setting off a chain reaction. The rest of the colony quickly knows of the danger.

Termites form head-banging chains to warn of predators.

Fish can feel the movement of other fish nearby.

Elephant
Communication

African elephants mostly live in family groups, ranging over the African **savannas.** These smart creatures have developed amazing ways of communicating in their groups, with other herds, and with elephants (usually males) that live alone. An elephant warns its herd of danger by trumpeting and stamping. At the same time, other herds, too far away to see or hear this, feel the vibrations through the ground, picking them up with their feet and also their trunks.

Trunks are very important to elephant communication. Elephants can touch them as a greeting; use them to nudge a calf along; or to feel or sniff a new object. The trunk is very sensitive to both touch and smells. Elephants make noises through their trunks— the famous trumpet, for example—and they use them to make visual signals. The position of an elephant's trunk and ears signal its emotional state. An elephant flaps its ears and raises its trunk as a greeting, but will make these gestures bigger to send a warning.

Elephants are like humans in their ability to communicate using all their senses. Scientists think that they can recognize up to 100 different elephant voices and can pick up infrasound over long distances. Elephants use many visual signals and

communicate through touch and taste. Smell is also of great importance—for example, both male and female elephants give out particular scents when they are ready to **mate.**

The saying "an elephant never forgets" has some truth. Elephants have the intelligence to learn and remember communication signals. There are many examples of elephants excitedly greeting each other after a long time apart. Elephants' ability to remember may also help them form close relationships in the herd. Elephants are known to comfort each other and seem sad when a member of the herd dies.

Studying Animal Communication

We know so much about how animals communicate because, over many years, **zoologists** have studied animals and kept a record of their signals and actions. These studies have often been conducted on animals in the wild, but they have also involved animals kept in zoos and laboratories.

PATIENCE AND TIME

Many scientists spend their whole lives studying a single **species.** Joyce Poole, a founder of a project called ElephantVoices, has spent over 35 years studying African elephants (see page 41) and how they communicate. She was inspired by Jane Goodall, a zoologist famous for her study of chimpanzees in the wild, which began in 1960. The Austrian scientist Karl von Frisch published his groundbreaking ideas on the bees' "waggle dance" (see page 14) in 1927 and continued his studies throughout his life, earning a Nobel Prize for his work in 1973.

RETHINKING OUR WORLD

Many people did not believe von Frisch's research when it was first published. They questioned how a simple creature like a bee could have developed such a complex form of communication. Yet his findings have been supported and built upon by many other scientists since then. The work of zoologists like this has not only grown our knowledge of animals, but also has encouraged people to value and respect these animals. Many zoologists have become involved in the fight to protect animals and the places in which they live from destruction by people.

Decoding a language

Dolphins have long fascinated scientists with their underwater whistles and clicks. Could this be a **language,** somewhat like those spoken by humans, with words and sentences? Scientists agree that dolphins certainly communicate with these sounds, and a few even claim to have found evidence of words. But most agree there is still a long way to go before humans can decode "dolphin."

Dolphins use sound to communicate.

The idea that bees communicate by dancing was considered quite strange in 1927.

Talking to Animals

Many humans not only wish to study how animals communicate but also to communicate with them. Such communication has happened naturally with the taming of animals. There is, for example, much communication between humans and their pets, and farmers often recognize and act on the various signals given out by their sheep and cows.

Dogs are descended from wolves and are naturally pack animals. For most pet dogs, the "pack" is the human family they live with. The study of wolves has helped humans communicate with and train their pet dogs. Just as wolves have **dominant** members of their pack, dogs may also look to and feel more secure with a leader—usually their owner. Dogs do not truly understand the word sit, but they do understand the tone of voice and signal that goes with it. They will usually respond best if the command is given by the dominant pack member.

Some scientists have tried to teach human **language** to animals in zoos. They found that chimpanzees and gorillas could be taught simple sign language and recognize and understand some words, such as water.

One of the best animal learners of human language was not an **ape,** but a parrot. African grey parrots are smart, social animals. One such parrot, named Alex, was trained to speak

more than 100 words and could tell apart colors, shapes, and materials. He could count up to seven and perform simple addition and subtraction problems. When looking in the mirror, Alex once asked, "What color?" referring to himself. In asking what color he was, he became the only nonhuman animal known to ask a question about itself.

Some people wonder if it is right to carry out these experiments. But when carried out ethically and with good research methods, they can teach us much about how language developed.

Glossary

antenna (plural antennae) a long, delicate sense organ, or feeler, found on the heads of various invertebrates, including insects.

ape a member of a small group of mammals most like humans that includes chimpanzees, gorillas, gibbons, and orangutans. Unlike monkeys, apes do not have a tail.

bioluminescent describing a light given off by such living things as glowworms and deep-sea fish. Bioluminescence is caused by a chemical reaction involving a light-emitting pigment—coloring—inside the creature.

colony a group of living things of one species that live together or grow in the same place.

courtship the behavior, often repeated, of animals in the lead-up to mating.

dominant having power or influence over another.

extinction when every member of a species (kind) of living thing has died.

foraging searching for food.

gland an organ in an animal's body that secretes (gives off) chemical substances for use in the body or for release into the surroundings.

grooming when an animal cleans its own or another's feathers, fur, or skin.

insect one of the major invertebrate groups. Insects have six legs and a three-part body.

invertebrate an animal without a backbone.

language a system of communication where signs or signals (such as sounds) are connected together to create a specific meaning.

larva (plural larvae) the active, immature stage of some animals, such as many insects, that is different from its adult form.

lateral line the system of sense organs possessed by fish that enables them to feel movement in the water.

mammal one of the major vertebrate animal groups. Mammals feed their offspring on milk produced by the mother, and most have hair or fur.

mate the animal with which another animal partners to reproduce; the act of mating, when two animals come together to reproduce.

mimic to copy something, or the close external resemblance of an animal to something else; an animal that does this.

musk a distinct scent given off by certain animals.

organ a part of the body, made of similar cells and cell tissue, that performs a particular function.

pheromone a chemical substance linked to the sense of smell given out by an animal as a signal to others in its species.

plumage a bird's feathers.

predator an animal that hunts, kills, and eats other animals.

preen in a bird, to clean its feathers.

prey an animal that is hunted, killed, and eaten by another.

reptile one of the major vertebrate animal groups. A reptile has dry, scaly skin and breathes air. Snakes, crocodiles, and lizards are all reptiles.

savanna grasslands with widely scattered bushes and trees.

school in fish, to move together in a large group through the water; a group of fish moving together through the water.

social structure a network of relationships among individual animals and groups of animals.

spawn to lay and fertilize eggs in water.

species a group of living things that have certain permanent traits in common and are able to reproduce with each other.

submission surrendering to a stronger or superior individual.

suckle to feed a young animal with milk from the breast or teat. Only mammals suckle their young.

swarm a large group of arthropods moving together either in search of food or a new home. An arthropod is an animal with jointed legs and no backbone.

swim bladder an organ in fish that helps them control the depth they float at in the water.

territory an area of land or water controlled by an animal or group of animals, which they defend from other animals.

venomous describes an animal that produces venom or a part of such an animal that releases venom. Venom is a naturally produced liquid that animals can introduce into other animals (for example, through biting) in order to stun, injure, or kill the other animal.

vertebrate an animal with a backbone.

voice box also called the larynx, the organ found in some animals, including humans, that enables them to make complex sounds.

zoologist a scientist who studies animals.

BOOKS

Amazing Animal Communicators (Animal Scientists) by Leon Gray (Capstone, 2015)

Dancing Bees and Other Amazing Communicators (Animal Superpowers) by Mary Lindeen (Lerner Classroom, 2017)

How and Why Do Animals Communicate? (All About Animals Close-up) by Bobbie Kalman (Crabtree Publishing Company, 2015)

Talk, Talk, Squawk! A Human's Guide to Animal Communication (Animal Science) by Nicola Davies (Candlewick, 2015)

WEBSITES

ElephantVoices
www.elephantvoices.org
The organization built around the research of Joyce Poole into how elephants communicate, including access to the huge database they have compiled of the different ways these animals communicate.

Jane Goodall Institute
www.janegoodall.org
Describes the work and research by Dr. Jane Goodall into chimpanzees, with information on the organization she founded to conserve them.

Ocean Mammal Institute
www.oceanmammalinst.org/songs.html
A website that enables you to listen to the songs of the humpback whale.

Index

African grey parrots 45
alarm calls 18, 19
alligators 28, 34
ants 30, 35

baboons 36, 37
bees 14, 30, 37, 42, 43
bioluminescence 9
birds 6, 7, 8, 10, 11, 12, 14, 16, 17, 20, 22, 36, 45
birdsong 16, 17, 20
boars, wild 30
body language 14, 37
body noises 22
breaching 27
butterflies 30–31

carp 30
cats 10, 14, 34, 36
chameleons 8, 9
chamois 32
chimpanzees 10, 12, 13, 42, 44
colors 6, 7, 8, 9
crickets 22
crocodiles 28, 34

dancing displays 14
dogs 12, 13, 28, 44, 45
dolphins 43

elephants 10, 24, 32, 34, 40–42
emotion, showing 8, 12, 13, 40, 41

facial expressions 12–13
fiddler crabs 11
fireflies 9
fish 8, 22–24, 30, 32–34, 38, 39
food, seeking 4, 10, 11, 14, 16, 30, 32

frogs 16, 17, 20, 38
    Caribbean white-lipped frogs 38
    poison dart frogs 6

gazelles 15
geese 20
giant cuttlefish 8
gibbons 21, 36
giraffes 34
gorillas 22, 44
greetings 34, 35, 40, 41
grooming 10, 36, 37

hearing 4, 16, 19, 24, 25
help, seeking 10, 12
hippos 24, 25
horses 13, 34, 35
hoverflies 7

iguanas 19
infrasound 24, 26, 40

ladybugs 6
lions 20, 21
location, communicating 20, 24, 27, 28

mammals 12, 35
mates, seeking 4, 6, 7, 8, 9, 10, 11, 14, 16, 17, 22, 24, 27, 28, 30–31, 32, 34, 38
mice 24, 25
monitor lizards 14, 15
moths 24, 32
movement 10
musk 28, 29
musk deer 29

orangutans 22

pheasants 7, 14
pheromones 30–31, 32
prairie dogs 18, 19
preening 36

rabbits 24
ravens 10
rhinos 28, 29

seahorses 34
sharks 32, 33
sight 4, 6, 13
smell, sense of 4, 28, 32, 33, 40, 41
snakes 20, 23, 24, 33
    rattlesnakes 23
spiders 38
stickleback 8

taste 4, 41
termites 39
territory, marking 4, 5, 14, 17, 20, 21, 22, 25
toadfish 22, 23
touch, sense of 4, 34, 40, 41
trickery 8

ultrasound 24, 25

vervet monkeys 18
vibrations 17, 22, 23, 25, 38, 40

warning of danger 4, 12, 18, 38, 39, 40
warning signals 6, 7, 9, 14, 20, 28, 30
whales 24, 26–27
    humpback whales 26, 27
wolves 5, 12, 32, 44
woodpeckers 22

www.ingramcontent.com/pod-product-compliance
Lightning Source LLC
Chambersburg PA
CBHW041043050726
47599CB00018B/2060